The
Lincolns

by
Cass R. Sandak

D1359951

CRESTWOOD HOUSE
New York

Maxwell Macmillan Canada
Toronto

Maxwell Macmillan International
New York Oxford Singapore Sydney

Library of Congress Cataloging-in-Publication Data
Sandak, Cass R.
    The Lincolns / by Cass R. Sandak. — 1st ed.
    p. cm. — (First families)
    Includes bibliographical references and index.
    Summary: Examines the family life and political career of Abraham Lincoln, with an emphasis on his
relationship with his wife.
    ISBN 0-89686-641-6
    1. Lincoln, Abraham, 1809–1865—Family—Juvenile literature. 2. Lincoln family—Juvenile literature.
3. Presidents—United States—Biography—Juvenile literature. 4. United States—History—Civil War, 1861–1865—
Juvenile literature. [1. Lincoln, Abraham, 1809–1865. 2. Lincoln, Mary Todd, 1818–1882. 3. Lincoln family.
4. Presidents. 5. First ladies.] I. Title. II. Series: Sandak, Cass R.   First families.
E457.905.S26   1992
973.7'0922—dc20
[B]   92-6880

Photo Credits
Cover: Ford's Theater—National Park Services
AP—Wide World Photos: 4, 7, 14, 17, 18, 21, 23, 37, 39, 44
The Bettmann Archive: 10, 25, 26, 29, 33, 35, 43
The Lincoln Museum, a part of Lincoln National Corporation: 6, 9, 30

Macmillan Publishing Company   Maxwell Macmillan Canada, Inc.
866 Third Avenue   1200 Eglinton Avenue East
New York, NY 10022   Suite 200
                                    Don Mills, Ontario M3C 3N1

CRESTWOOD HOUSE

Macmillan Publishing Company is part of the Maxwell Communication Group of Companies.

Produced by Flying Fish Studio

Printed in the United States of America

First edition

10 9 8 7 6 5 4 3 2 1

Contents

One of the few known photographs of Lincoln delivering the Gettysburg Address

A Splendid Speech

In 1863 the Civil War had been raging for two years. A great country had been torn in half. North fought South. On July 1, in the small Pennsylvania town of Gettysburg, one of the most devastating battles of the war began. Four days later it was over. The Union had won a major victory, but at a very great cost. More than 50,000 soldiers on both sides had been killed or wounded.

In November of that year, President Abraham Lincoln was asked to go to Gettysburg and help dedicate the cemetery at the battlefield where so many had fallen. The president's wife, Mary Todd Lincoln, had been planning to go with her husband. But at the last minute their son Tad took sick and she remained at home to look after him.

On November 19, 1863, crowds arrived. The people listened while the keynote speaker, Edward Everett, droned on for two hours. Then President Lincoln stood up and delivered what has come to be known as the Gettysburg Address.

It was a brief speech. In fact it is less than 300 words long and took only two minutes to deliver. Lincoln worked very hard to make its simple words reflect just the right tone.

5

Lincoln collected his thoughts before he left Washington, D.C. He then drafted the speech on the back of an envelope while the train sped him the 200 miles from the nation's capital to Gettysburg. Even on the morning he was to deliver the speech he was still making small changes to get the wording just right.

And then he spoke the words: "Fourscore and seven years ago . . ."

It had been a long journey for Abraham Lincoln to that momentous day.

The log cabin in which Abraham Lincoln was born in 1809

Thomas Lincoln

Young Abe

Abraham Lincoln's father was named Thomas Lincoln. He was a farmer and carpenter and member of the Kentucky militia. In 1806 he married a woman named Nancy Hanks. Almost nothing is known about her except that by family tradition she had come from Virginia to Kentucky. Lincoln believed, however, that his mother came from a distinguished family. Both parents were unable to sign their names, and it is probable that they could neither read nor write. The couple settled in Kentucky, near Little Pigeon Creek. The Lincolns' first child was a daughter named Nancy but called Sarah. She was born in 1807.

Abraham was their second-born child. He was named after his grandfather Lincoln. Abraham was born February 12, 1809, in a one-room log cabin near Hodgenville, Kentucky. The cabin measured 18 feet by 16 feet. It had one window, one door and a dirt floor. The Lincolns had one more child, a son named Thomas. Born in 1811, he died shortly after.

Abraham's relationship with his father was strained. It is probable that their personalities conflicted. Young Abe was intense and ambitious, whereas by all accounts his father was very easygoing.

One of Abraham's best friends was Dennis Hanks. He was the adopted son of Nancy Hanks Lincoln's aunt and uncle. At six, Abraham attended a so-called blab school. There were no books of any kind, so the students just recited, or "blabbed," all their lessons out loud after the teacher instructed them. Some things sank in, while others did not. Abe's formal schooling lasted a total of one year.

When Abe was seven, the family moved from Kentucky to Indiana. In 1818 Nancy Hanks Lincoln died. Abe was only nine, but he had to help his father build a coffin for his dead mother. Sarah tried to be both mother and sister to young Abe, but she herself was only 11. (Sarah was not very strong. She died in childbirth in 1828 when she was only 20 years old.)

Without his wife, Tom Lincoln was a lonely man. He made a trip back to Kentucky. There he met a woman who would become his new wife. Tom Lincoln returned to Indiana with the woman. The lady's name was Sarah (or Sally) Bush Johnston. She was a widow who already had three children of her own.

After the wedding, Abe became more attached to his stepmother than he was to his own father. She was a cheerful woman who encouraged the young boy to read as much as possible. Although Abe had little schooling, he could read from an early age and did so eagerly. As a

Lincoln's stepmother at the age of 76

youngster he read accounts of the lives of George Washington and Thomas Jefferson. He admired both men—and their achievements—tremendously.

Another of Abe's favorites was Daniel Defoe's *Robinson Crusoe*. He did not have access to many books, so those he did have he read over and over. Like most pioneering families, the Lincolns found the Bible a major source of inspiration. Abraham learned many passages from the Scriptures by heart. Later he wrote, "Take all the Bible that you can on reason, and the rest on faith." Abe Lincoln was not a member of any church. But he attended services and believed in God.

Abraham Lincoln as a rail-splitter, one of many physically demanding jobs the young man worked

With little education and no social advantages, Lincoln had to make his way in the world through physical labor. At 17 he began to work on the Ohio River, using a small boat that he owned. With this boat he carried people ashore from the larger boats that moved passengers and freight up and down the river.

When Abe was 19 he went south to New Orleans with a load of produce that he hoped to sell at a profit. He expected to make the city his home. He also earned money swinging an ax. With his ax he split rails for the new railroads that were being built all across the country in the mid-19th century. But he soon grew homesick.

The Move to Illinois

In 1830 Abraham Lincoln turned 21. The next year, when he was 22, Lincoln moved to New Salem, Illinois. He stayed there six years, and from this point on he began to consider Illinois his home.

By this time Lincoln was almost six feet five inches tall and was lean and gangly. He seemed even taller than he was because he was so thin and his legs were very long. Possessed of a good sense of humor, he was also intelligent and ambitious. He was always thinking and always looking for ways to improve himself. We would probably describe Abe Lincoln as distant and absentminded. He often wrote notes to himself and kept them hidden under his stovepipe hat.

In his early twenties Lincoln first became interested in local politics. He joined the New Salem militia in 1832 to fight Native Americans. He was elected captain of his unit. It was the first time that people recognized Lincoln's leadership abilities. But, ironically, during the entire campaign, Lincoln never even saw any Native Americans.

In an effort to establish himself, Lincoln became a partner in a general-store venture. Lincoln's partner was never very healthy. His early death left Lincoln owing a large number of debts and holding an unsuccessful store. In order to eke out a living, Lincoln also served as a postmaster and surveyor while he farmed.

In 1834 Lincoln was elected to serve a two-year term in the Illinois House of Representatives. Because he was torn between politics and a career in law, Lincoln taught himself the legal profession as well. He believed that lawyers had many opportunities to work for the good of both society and individuals. Absentminded he may have been, but Lincoln was obviously methodical and cool as well.

Lincoln was in his mid-twenties when he became friendly with a young lady named Ann Rutledge. She was the daughter of a friend. But the friendship did not last, as she took sick and died at 22. Legend says that Lincoln took her death particularly hard. People speculated that the two were romantically involved, but this was probably not true. There is no evidence to show that Rutledge and Lincoln were anything other than close friends.

Lincoln did have a strange courtship with a woman named Mary Owen, but nothing much came of it. In general, Lincoln was not considered a good catch by most women or by their families. Although he was intelligent and a good speaker, he had no education and no settled profession. And his prospects were not thought to be very bright.

But Lincoln was forging a career for himself in politics. He was easily reelected to the Illinois House of Representatives in 1836, 1838 and 1840. This gave him a total of eight years, or four terms, as a state lawmaker.

Settling in Springfield

In 1840, when Lincoln was 31, he moved from New Salem to Springfield, Illinois. Here he set up a law practice with a partner, John Todd Stuart. In 1837, after studying intensively for three years, Lincoln had passed the necessary exams that allowed him to practice law.

Lincoln kept establishing himself as a name in politics and was also becoming more and more well known as a lawyer. In 1840 Lincoln defended his first case before the Illinois Supreme Court.

Young Mary Todd

In 1839 Lincoln met a charming young woman at a dance in Springfield. Her name was Mary Todd and she was nine years younger than Lincoln. He was then 30 years old. They began a relaxed and devoted courtship. His nickname for her was Molly. The two soon reached an understanding that someday they would get married. In essence, they became engaged.

Mary's parents, Robert Smith Todd and Eliza Parker, had been pioneer settlers in Kentucky, but they quickly helped form the ranks of high society in the fast-developing Kentucky city of Lexington. Festive parties and balls and long visits by relatives formed the backdrop of young Mary Todd's upbringing.

Mary Todd had been born into this kind of luxury on December 13, 1818. She was only seven when her mother died. Like Lincoln's father, Robert Todd soon remarried. Mary had been well educated by tutors at home. Unlike many of her contemporaries, she even spoke French. At 14 Mary was sent off to finishing school. But by the time she was 18 she was to recall her childhood as lonely and desolate.

Young Mary Todd

Mary and her stepmother did not get along well. There was no active dislike on the part of either woman, but the sensitive Mary felt unwelcome in her stepmother's home. She had two older sisters living in Springfield, Illinois. So she moved there to be close to them—and away from her stepmother.

Mary Todd was a friendly and vivacious young woman who had plenty of suitors. One was a friend of Lincoln's, Stephen A. Douglas. The match with Lincoln was opposed by Mary's father and her sister. The Todds were well-to-do people, and Mary had been raised in a very different way than Abe Lincoln had been. The Todds simply felt that Abe Lincoln wasn't good enough for Mary.

Mary Todd was a petite five feet two inches tall. She had clear blue eyes with long lashes and hair that was light brown with darker highlights. She impressed people with her intelligence and wit. But in her quickness to size people up, she was sometimes thoughtlessly sarcastic.

In many ways, even as an adult, Mary Todd resembled a child. Her short stature and plumpness, offset with fussy gowns, gave the grown woman a doll-like appearance. This was only reinforced by her capricious ways. She was vain and extravagant. She found most photographs of herself unflattering.

Mary's wealthy background allowed her to indulge a liking for nice clothes and fashionable accessories. In a time when department stores were just coming into existence, Mary loved to spend time visiting specialty shops that carried fine merchandise. Nothing pleased Mary more than a shopping expedition during which she could spend plenty of money on dresses, shoes, bonnets and gloves.

Lincoln went to special lengths to hide his humble beginnings. He hardly kept in touch with his father and stepmother. And he took great pains to keep his early life a secret from almost everyone.

Eventually Mary's sister and brother-in-law, Mr. and Mrs. Ninian Edwards, talked Mary into breaking her "understanding" with Lincoln. Lincoln became depressed. Mary, too, was unhappy. Eventually they began to write to each other and then, cautiously, to meet from time to time. They realized after all that they really were in love with each other and decided to set a wedding date.

The Happy Couple

On November 4, 1842, after a stressful courtship that had lasted three years, Abraham Lincoln and Mary Todd became husband and wife. Lincoln did not tell his family. Mary did tell hers, and the Todds finally gave in and granted their blessing. But she didn't tell them until the morning of the wedding. So, they had no choice but to accept Mary's decision. The wedding cake was even baked at her sister's home.

The Lincolns' married life did not begin smoothly. Mary continued her passion for fine clothes and spending money. And Abe unfortunately was still trying to pay off some early debts. When they were first married they lived above the Globe Tavern in Springfield. It wasn't the kind of address Mary was used to, but the Lincolns were very much in love.

The Lincolns' first year of marriage—living above the tavern—was very hard on the couple. They were poor and Mary was not used to doing things for herself. After all, she had grown up in a well-to-do family in Kentucky. There had always been slaves on hand to help out. Mary wasn't used to sacrificing herself to anything—especially not poverty.

Sometimes Mary grew weary of her husband's coarse ways. And sometimes she lost her temper and shrieked loudly at everyone. But Lincoln was patient with her. He knew that if he let her blow off steam, she would be fine in a little while. Despite Mary's troubled personality, the

Lincolns' love for each other helped them overcome their differences. The newlyweds always managed to get along.

The Lincolns' first son was born on August 1, 1843, in the rooms above the tavern. He was named Robert Todd Lincoln. Not long after Robert's birth, the Lincolns bought a charming house in Springfield. As it turned out, it was the only house the Lincolns ever owned. The couple's second son was born on March 10, 1846. He was named Edward Baker Lincoln.

The Lincolns' house in Springfield, Illinois

17

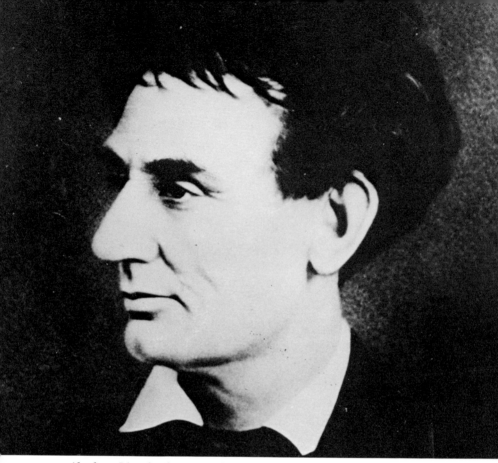

Abraham Lincoln, four years before being elected president

A Rising Star
in Politics

During much of the 1840s, family life and the practice of law occupied most of Lincoln's time. In 1843 he failed to gain the Whig nomination to the U.S. House of Representatives. He tried again in 1846 and finally succeeded. In 1847 the Lincolns saw Washington, D.C., for the first time. They had moved there so Lincoln could serve his term. Their home was a rented house.

Mary Todd Lincoln found Washington particularly disagreeable, and after only a short time she and their sons left. Part of the problem was that they did not yet have sufficient income to keep up with the lifestyle they saw around them. Some extremely tender correspondence between the two survives from this period of geographic separation. Mary didn't really like being alone, and she found that she needed her husband to make her life complete.

Lincoln stayed by himself. He delivered the so-called Polk oration, named after President James K. Polk. In it, Lincoln spoke out against the U.S. war against Mexico, which had begun in April 1846. The speech was not popular. Other politicians used it to discredit Lincoln. Largely because of the sentiments Lincoln expressed in the speech, he was not reelected to Congress in 1848. As a result, he withdrew from politics for a time. He returned quietly to Springfield and for the next five years concentrated on his law practice and on raising his family.

The Lincolns' son Eddie died on February 1, 1850. He was not yet four years old. Some people cannot accept this kind of tragedy with ease. Mary Lincoln was one of those people. She spent much of her time weeping, on the verge of hysterics. In December of that same year, Mary Lincoln gave birth to another son, William Wallace, known as Willie. And on April 4, 1853, their last child, another son, was born. He was named Thomas but was called Taddie or Tad.

The Problem of Slavery

Slavery was an issue that was causing great differences between the North and South. By the early 1850s there were several million slaves in the United States, mostly in the South.

The North was largely industrial—and becoming even more so. The farms there were mostly small, so there was very little need for slaves. In addition, the strong religious beliefs against slavery that were prevalent in the North helped to contain the problem there. Northern abolitionists were people who believed in ending, or abolishing, slavery.

The South was much more rural, but its farms, or plantations, were large. The population there was about half the size of the North's. Its economy was almost entirely agricultural so there was always a huge demand for both paid and slave labor.

Some members of the Whig party were particularly strong believers in the antislavery movement. They broke off from the Whigs, along with some Democrats, and formed the Republican party. Lincoln joined them.

The Republican party in Illinois nominated Lincoln in 1858 to be a candidate for the U.S. Senate. It was during this period that Lincoln delivered what came to be known as the "House Divided" speech. In it, he implored the nation to remain together. There could be no future in a country that was half slave and half free: "A house divided against itself cannot stand." And fall it soon did.

During the 1858 campaign for the U.S. Senate seat from Illinois, the Lincoln-Douglas debates were set up. Stephen A. Douglas was an old friend of Lincoln's (and a former suitor of Mary's). But over the years their beliefs had caused a serious division. Douglas was a staunch Democrat, and now they were political rivals. Lincoln opposed slavery in new territories; Douglas did not. Douglas was strongly racist.

Running for the same Senate seat, both candidates agreed to debate their differences of opinion publicly. A series of seven debates were scheduled in different Illinois cities. Each debate lasted about three hours. The debates gained a great deal of publicity both for the issues and for Lincoln and Douglas. (Because of her duties as a mother, Mary Lincoln was only able to attend the final debate.)

The Lincoln-Douglas debates made both men better known to the public.

People came from great distances to hear the two distinguished orators. Because of great public interest and heavy newspaper coverage, both men became even better known than previously.

Lincoln lost his Senate bid by only a small number of votes. He may have become depressed by the defeat, but he learned much by trial and error and never made the same mistake twice.

A New President

Having tasted public acclaim and come close to victory, Lincoln decided to make a bid for the White House in 1860. The Republican party obliged by naming him as their candidate for president at the Republican National Convention in May of that year. It was during this period that Lincoln's image as "Honest Abe" became a campaign slogan. It was not a nickname with which Lincoln was very comfortable. He thought it undignified and unsophisticated. Perhaps it even reminded him too much of his humble beginnings.

The Democratic party chose Stephen A. Douglas as Lincoln's opposition. This was the very same man who had opposed him two years earlier in the Senate race. This time Douglas was the Democratic presidential candidate, while Lincoln stood for the Republican party. It marked only the second time a candidate for president had run on the Republican party ticket.

Lincoln was elected 16th president of the United States on November 6, 1860. He carried 40 percent of the popular

A picture used on a poster during Lincoln's campaign for the presidency

vote and 60 percent of the electoral college vote. Not surprisingly—because his antislavery stand was so strong—Lincoln carried 18 of the 22 northern states.

The South was outraged by Lincoln's election. Lincoln opposed slavery, and slavery was considered essential to the economy of the South. Just a month after Lincoln's election, South Carolina seceded from, or left, the Union. The United States were no longer united. It appeared that something serious was about to happen.

The Lincolns left Springfield for Washington, D.C., in February 1861. Lincoln had spent more than 25 years of his life in the Illinois town. Because the train made many stops, the trip was a long one. Despite death threats and warnings, Mary and the children accompanied Lincoln on the journey. The family enjoyed the trappings of the luxurious presidential car. There are accounts, however, of how mischievous the children were.

On March 4, 1861, Lincoln was inaugurated as president of the United States. The unfinished dome of the Capitol was not yet in place. The day ended with an inaugural ball. At one point, Mary Lincoln danced with Stephen Douglas, her old beau and her husband's "enemy." Lincoln himself did not attend the ball. And that night the Lincolns slept for the first time in the White House.

Even before inauguration day, more states had seceded to form the Confederate States of America (CSA) under the leadership of Jefferson Davis. The future of a unified America seemed in doubt.

Lincoln had been in office less than six weeks on April 12, 1861, when the first shots were exchanged between North and South. On that day, Confederate forces attacked Union ships at Fort Sumter, near Charleston, South Carolina. The Civil War had begun.

The North consisted of 22 states and some 22 million people; the South was made up of 11 states with nine million people. The North also had the skills of a developing economy. But the South had highly trained and dedicated military forces, while the North's leaders were merely adequate.

The Wartime White House

The first battle in the war occurred at Bull Run, Virginia (or Manassas, as it was called by Southerners). It was a clear victory for the Confederates. The results also served notice that the war was going to be a tougher and longer one than anyone had at first thought. Because Bull Run was so close to Washington, D.C., the Lincoln family could hear the roar of cannon fire as the battle took place. From the White House windows Lincoln could see returning soldiers when the battle was over. Guards stood nearby in case the city was besieged, but this never occurred.

Lincoln spent as much time as possible with his family, but the demands of his office often called him away.

As president, Lincoln became commander in chief of the Union, in accordance with the Constitution, even though he had virtually no military experience. While Lincoln was at the head of the army, his young children were still boys playing soldier in the White House.

Both Willie and Taddie were the first young children of a president to live in the executive mansion. The whole mansion became their playground. Often their pet goat could be seen rampaging through business offices. They especially loved the building's huge, flat roof, where they could reenact their own Civil War battles. They also discovered the servants' bell system and played havoc both with it and with the servants.

Personal tragedy struck the Lincolns again in early 1862. Both boys fell ill, and 11-year-old Willie died on February 20. Willie Lincoln's funeral was held in the White House. The body was laid out in the Green Room before burial. Without question, Willie had been Mary Lincoln's favorite. The death of this second child upset Mary Lincoln a great deal, but the public felt that her hysteria was uncalled for. Grief was one thing, but there was no reason for a public figure to carry on so.

After Willie's death, Mary Lincoln became very nervous and suspicious of everyone. In an effort to find some comfort, she experimented with spiritualism. On more than one occasion, both Lincolns attended seances. From that time on, the shopping and spending that Mary Lincoln enjoyed so much became an obsession. There are records showing that she purchased 300 pairs of gloves in a single month.

Tad Lincoln, dressed in a colonel's uniform, loved playing Civil War games with his brother Willie.

As a Southerner, Mary was eyed with distrust by many people. One full brother and several half brothers were fighting in the Confederate army. And many of her Southern relatives were killed during the course of the war. Some people even said she was a spy for the Southern forces. But there is no evidence that this was true.

Life with the Lincolns

The White House was so close to the battle lines of the Civil War that danger lurked in every corner. From the White House, the president could see soldiers' campfires in Virginia. He could also see the Confederate flags waving over nearby Alexandria, Virginia.

The Lincolns were given a standard $20,000 for repairs when they came to the White House, but Mary Lincoln soon went over budget. Despite the war, she carried out a great deal of redecoration in the house. Upholstery, velvet wallpaper, lavish curtains and draperies were added to the furnishings. Significant changes were made to the Red, Green, Blue and East rooms. On February 5, 1862, these newly decorated rooms were all open for display and the public was invited to a reception.

Although there is now a Lincoln bedroom in the White House, it was never actually slept in by the Lincolns. It was, in fact, created after the Lincoln years. Measuring only 16 feet by 13 feet, it was the room where Lincoln held cabinet meetings.

Later on the room became a bedroom. Because some of the Lincoln family furniture was used to decorate the room, it has become known as the Lincoln bedroom. Many of Lincoln's personal effects eventually found their way into the room. More recently, President Richard M. Nixon used the room as a retreat away from the noise and bustle of the rest of the White House.

Lincoln rose early and usually had breakfast with his family around eight o'clock. Most days he would already have done some important work before joining his family. He was a light eater. Eggs and coffee were his usual breakfast. Then he would work for another hour before welcom-

A family portrait of the Lincolns. Robert Lincoln, shown standing, graduated from Harvard and joined the Union army.

A White House reception

ing the round of callers. These people came for meetings with the president between ten o'clock and one o'clock. Then he rejoined his family for a modest lunch.

The hours until four o'clock were given over to writing speeches and signing documents. At four he and his wife would get into a carriage and go for a ride around the nation's capital. Dinner was served around six o'clock. After dinner Lincoln tried to keep evenings free to spend time with his family, but frequently he had to return to work.

Because Lincoln knew almost nothing about military leadership, he spent a great deal of time at the White House studying volumes on war strategies. It was a short walk across the White House to the offices of the War Department. There he would receive the latest war news from the various battlefields.

Mary Lincoln took extremely good care of both her husband and their sons. But in the public eye, she could not do anything right. During the war, she felt that receptions to keep people's spirits up should be held as scheduled. Some thought she was right, but others criticized her for being frivolous in the face of the devastation around her.

Mary Lincoln turned out to be a gracious and witty hostess who always managed to put her guests at ease. While he was president, Lincoln said of her: "My wife is as handsome as when she was a girl and I fell in love with her; and what is more, I have never fallen out."

The War Goes On

The war continued at its slow pace. Many people felt that Lincoln could have speeded up the end of the war. The South continued to demonstrate superior military leadership. At the same time, the Union army couldn't muster the strength it needed to put down the Southern forces effectively. Lincoln finally dismissed General George McClellan in November 1862. And in 1862 Lincoln ordered the Union army to attack Richmond, Virginia. As the capital of the Confederacy, Richmond was a Southern stronghold.

Lincoln was so involved in the Civil War that he spent almost no time on foreign affairs. During his term of office, almost no domestic issues—besides the problem of slavery—were given any attention.

Although Lincoln was really a moderate in his views, he began to see the South in a very unfavorable light. To Lincoln it seemed that the South would not give way on any point. The South made the idea of any compromise impossible. The war would have to be a fight to the finish.

The Emancipation Proclamation

On January 1, 1863, the Lincolns held a reception at the White House. Mary Lincoln was seen in public for the first time in almost a year. During the day, Lincoln went into an office on the second floor of the White House. Many years later the room would be known as the Lincoln bedroom.

A painting of Lincoln reading the Emancipation Proclamation to his cabinet

There he signed the Emancipation Proclamation. While the document did not actually free all slaves, it did release about 200,000 Southern slaves. Not all Northerners agreed with the Emancipation Proclamation. Many, especially Democrats, felt that blacks should not be freed. And others thought the document did not go far enough.

The document decreed that on January 1, 1863, the slaves in the Southern states were freed. There were obviously humanitarian reasons for doing this, but there were practical ones as well. Lincoln knew that many of the freed slaves would join the Union forces. And the army could use the soldiers. Despite having fought for nearly two years, the South was still stronger in military matters.

As a proclamation, the document was legally binding only in areas under military rule. It was only two years later, in 1865, that the 13th Amendment to the Constitution was signed and the proclamation became law. This amendment gave freedom to all Americans regardless of their color.

While the war raged on, Lincoln managed to spend time with his family at the White House. The only happy hours Lincoln spent during the Civil War were with his family. But without his brother Willie as playmate, young Taddie was lonely. Meanwhile, the Lincolns' oldest son, Robert, graduated from Harvard University in 1864. He then joined the Union army as a captain.

Although Mary Lincoln grew increasingly eccentric, her husband took good care of her. She suffered from severe migraine headaches, and her behavior became more and more unpredictable. On many occasions both Lincolns tried to cheer the wounded with hospital visits. Mary Lincoln even visited some hospitals on her own. It helped her pass the time and improved her spirits. It also helped convince the public that she had some interest in the war effort. Sometimes the couple would go together to the Retired Soldiers' Home, north of the city.

The War Is Over!

After two years, Lincoln finally found the right military leader to head the Union forces. Ulysses S. Grant was appointed and turned out to be the person the North needed to defeat the South. In some quarters, the name U. S. Grant stood for "Unconditional Surrender" Grant.

Abraham Lincoln, the strain of war visible in his face

As the war dragged on, a new election came up in 1864. Only shortly before election day did it become clear that the Union was actually winning the war. Largely as a result, Lincoln won a majority of both the popular vote and the votes of the electoral college. There were about four million votes cast for him; he won by a margin of half a million of those. Oddly enough, Lincoln's opponent on the ticket was the general he had dismissed just a few years before, George McClellan.

On March 4, 1865, Lincoln's second inauguration was held. Lincoln and his son Tad visited Richmond in early April. They found there wasn't much left of the city. Finally, on April 9, General Robert E. Lee surrendered to General Ulysses S. Grant at a courthouse in Appomattox, Virginia. The war that had divided the nation was over. Four long years had passed. More than 600,000 soldiers had died or had been wounded.

On April 11 the surrender was celebrated in Washington, D.C. Anyone who wanted to visit the White House that day could. No special invitations were needed.

Many people gathered in front of the White House. They were eager to see President Lincoln and they wanted to hear him speak. Lincoln did not disappoint the crowd. He stepped in front of a window in the White House and spoke briefly to the gathered throng. Lincoln told the crowd that he would welcome the Southern states back into the Union without bitterness.

Our American Cousin

On April 14 the Lincolns went to Ford's Theater in Washington to see a new play, *Our American Cousin*. More than 1,700 people were jammed into the theater to see the popular piece. The audience was larger than usual that night because it was known that the Lincolns would be at the theater.

A popular actor, John Wilkes Booth, was a true Southerner. From the early days of the Civil War he had been eager to further the Confederate cause. As a result he was furious at Lincoln over the Union victory. He too joined the audience that night.

During the early part of the evening a bodyguard was positioned outside the president's box. But sometime during the performance the guard decided he wanted to see the play. Leaving his post, he took an empty seat and watched the performance. During the third act Booth was able to wander into the box. He then shot Lincoln in the back of the head while the actors were onstage. Booth escaped, but his shot was a good one. The bullet struck behind Lincoln's left ear and lodged in his brain. There was no way he could survive.

The president was carried to William Peterson's boardinghouse across the street from the theater. He was so tall that he had to be laid diagonally across the bed. There, at 7:22 A.M. the next morning, Abraham Lincoln died. Only ten hours had passed. The 56-year-old Lincoln was the first American president to be assassinated.

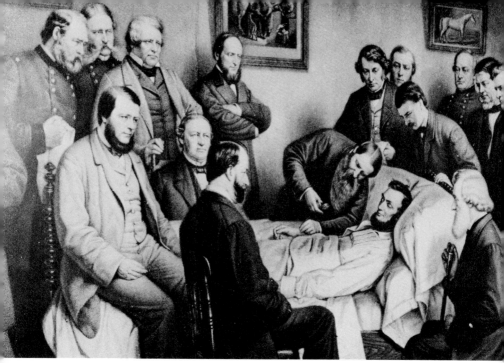

A painting of Lincoln on his deathbed

John Wilkes Booth broke his leg as he fled from Ford's Theater. Nonetheless, with help he managed to escape. It took authorities 12 days to find Booth. He was captured in a Virginia barn and immediately shot. Investigations later showed that Booth had been planning for some time to take Lincoln's life.

The Funeral

The funeral arrangements for the slain president were dignified and formal. Condolences poured in from around the world, and prominent figures made speeches about the president. When he heard of Lincoln's death, Secretary of War Edwin M. Stanton said, "Now he belongs to the ages."

This was the first time that an American president's funeral had been held in the White House. Mary Lincoln was so distraught that she was unable to help plan the funeral. The only decision she did make was that her husband's body would be returned to Illinois for burial in Springfield.

First Lincoln's body lay in state in the East Room of the White House. By the morning of April 18 a mile-long

Lincoln's funeral procession

39

crowd was waiting to file past and pay their respects. Some people waited up to six hours to get in. The room and its furnishings, including the pictures, mirrors and fireplace, were draped in black.

More than 100,000 spectators watched Lincoln's body being carried by a horse-drawn caisson from the White House to the Capitol. The procession itself was so long that it took two hours to pass any given point. Mary Lincoln remained in her White House bedroom, too grief-stricken to attend the ceremony. In the Capitol rotunda, some 3,000 people an hour filed past the coffin.

On April 21 the train bearing Lincoln's body began its long, slow journey back to Springfield. All along the route people lined the railroad tracks. The train stopped in 11 key cities along the way. They were the same cities where Lincoln's train had stopped on its way from Springfield to Washington just a little over four years earlier. At these points the train stopped, the coffin was unloaded, and the casket was carried on an elaborate bier to a suitable spot for people to pay their respects. It is estimated that more than one million people viewed the body on the journey.

Finally, on May 4, 1865, Lincoln's body was taken off the train in Springfield. And then it was buried in the town he had called his home for so many years.

For several weeks after Lincoln's death, Mary Lincoln remained in the White House. In fact she did not leave until May 22. And because she was so unpopular, there were the usual rumors surrounding her departure. This time, it was suggested that she had packed up much of the White House furniture to take with her. In reality, the public had such access to the mansion that it would have been simple for souvenir hunters to make off with almost any object.

Premonitions of Death

In retrospect, it is not surprising that Lincoln lost his life. Both Mary and Abe Lincoln received many hate letters when they lived in the White House. Even before the Lincolns had left Springfield in February 1861, Mary Lincoln had received a disturbing "gift." It was a painting of her husband that showed him with a rope around his neck. It was typical of the strong sentiments that Lincoln aroused.

In 1862 an attempt was made on Lincoln's life. But the shot only knocked off Lincoln's top hat. During the Civil War, the fighting was so close to Washington that often the White House itself was almost turned into a fortress. A shell could easily have killed the president and his family if the fighting had come closer.

The Lincolns had even received death threats from time to time. Some say Lincoln had received as many as 80 different letters that contained strong threats. Even on Lincoln's journey from Springfield to his first inauguration in Washington, a death threat had been made. Guards had secretly taken Lincoln off the train in Philadelphia, Pennsylvania. They had received word that an attempt would be made on the president's life in Baltimore, Maryland. The safest thing to do was to get Lincoln to Washington quickly—and under cover.

Even more astonishing was Lincoln's own premonition that he was going to be murdered. This came to him in a dream shortly before the assassination. In it, Lincoln dreamed that his funeral would be held in the East Room of the White House. And this is exactly what did happen.

Mary Lincoln Alone

After her husband's death, Mary Lincoln went into seclusion. For a time she traveled in Europe with her son Tad. But Tad died at 18 on July 15, 1871. It was the final blow for a seriously disturbed woman. Mary lost her reason. She believed she was penniless and had delusions that people were trying to kill her. A court hearing declared her insane. For a period of time she was institutionalized. About a year later the same court decided she was sane and she was released.

Certainly the evidence that Mary Lincoln suffered a serious mental disorder and was a danger to herself or others was very slim. Some historians now believe that the unfavorable ruling at her first sanity hearing had been engineered by Lincoln's enemies in an attempt to discredit the slain president and his family.

Mary Todd Lincoln was misunderstood in her own time and by history. Modern psychologists have suggested that she suffered from manic depression, a disorder characterized by alternating mood swings. Surely the tragic events of her life appear to have left her devastated, and she drifted in and out of a dreamy world of illusion.

After her husband's death, Mary Lincoln's mental condition worsened.

43

44

Mary Lincoln's final days were spent comfortably in the Springfield home of her sister Mrs. Ninian Edwards. This was the same house she had been living in when she became Lincoln's bride some 40 years before. She died on July 16, 1882, and she was laid to rest beside her husband in the Springfield cemetery.

Mary Lincoln's only surviving son, Robert Todd Lincoln, lived until 1926. He was secretary of war under presidents James Garfield and Chester Alan Arthur. A wealthy man, Robert Lincoln lived a long and distinguished life.

Robert Lincoln attending the dedication of the Lincoln Memorial

For Further Reading

Anthony, Carl Sferrazza. *First Ladies: The Saga of the Presidents' Wives and Their Power, 1789–1961.* New York: William Morrow and Company, Inc., 1990.

Fisher, Leonard Everett. *The White House.* New York: Holiday House, 1989.

Freedman, Russell. *Lincoln: A Photobiography.* New York: Clarion Books, 1987.

Friedel, Frank. *The Presidents of the United States of America.* Revised edition. Washington, D.C.: The White House Historical Association, 1989.

Klapthor, Margaret Brown. *The First Ladies.* Revised edition. Washington, D.C.: The White House Historical Association, 1989.

The Living White House. Revised edition. Washington, D.C.: The White House Historical Association, 1987.

Randall, Ruth Painter. *I Mary. A Biography of the Girl Who Married Abraham Lincoln.* Boston: Little, Brown & Co., 1959.

St. George, Judith. *The White House: Cornerstone of a Nation.* New York: G. P. Putnam's Sons, 1990.

Sandburg, Carl. *Abe Lincoln Grows Up.* New York: Harcourt, Brace and World, 1926, 1928.

Stefoff, Rebecca. *Abraham Lincoln: 16th President of the United States.* Ada, Oklahoma: Garrett Educational Corporation, 1989.

Taylor, Tim. *The Book of Presidents.* New York: Arno Press (A New York Times Company), 1972.

Index